Contents

Animals 2
The Loch Ness monster 4
Does the monster exist? 6
Where the monster may hide 8
Looking for the monster 10
Loch Ness 14
Glossary 16

ANIMALS

There are lots and lots of animals – big ones, small ones, hairy ones and smooth ones.

Do you know what these animals are?

All these animals exist. Some live in the sea. Some live on the land.

THE LOCH NESS MONSTER

Do you know what this animal is?
Some people say that it lives in a deep lake in Scotland.
The lake is called Loch Ness.

The animal is called the Loch Ness monster.

What does the Loch Ness monster look like? Some people say that it looks like a snake.

It is big and smooth. It is long and thin.

DOES THE MONSTER EXIST?

Many people have looked for the Loch Ness monster. Most of them have not seen it.

A lot of people say that the monster does not exist.

But maybe the monster does exist. Maybe it can hide well. Maybe it hides at the bottom of the lake.

WHERE THE MONSTER MAY HIDE

Some people say that it hides in a cave.
They say that it hides in a cave at the side of the lake.

They also say that the Loch Ness monster can dive.
It can dive very deep and very fast to hide in its cave.

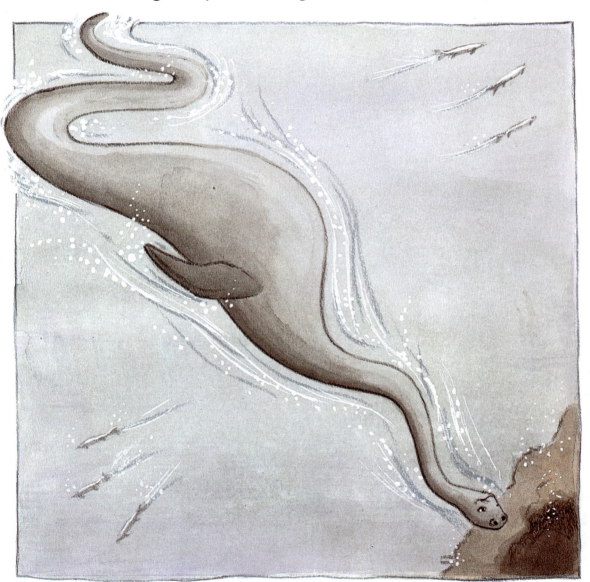

LOOKING FOR THE MONSTER

Many people go to Loch Ness. They go there to look for the monster. They want to find out if the monster exists.

What do people do to find out if the monster exists?
Some people watch the lake.

They watch it for a long, long time.

Some people go onto the lake in a boat.
They look for the monster from the boat.

Some people dive into the lake to look for the monster. They want to find out if the monster is at the bottom of the lake.

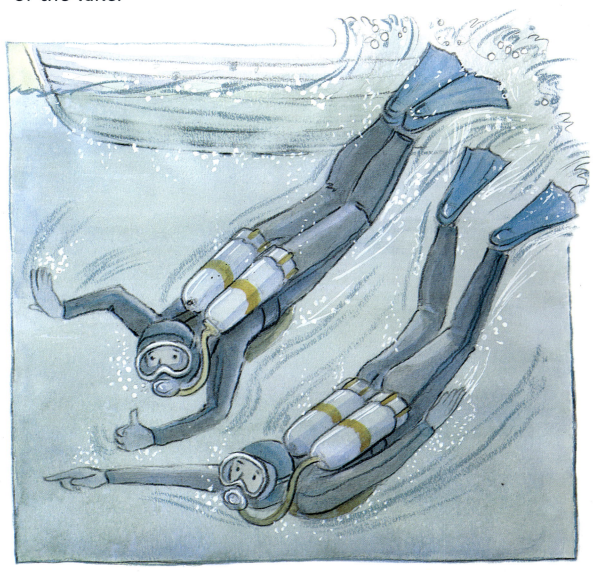

LOCH NESS

Loch Ness is a very, very deep lake. It is a very, very dark lake. It is hard to look for a monster in a deep, dark lake.

What do you think? Do you think there is a monster in Loch Ness? Does the Loch Ness monster exist?

Glossary

boat

bottom

cave

dive

hairy

hide

lake

smooth

snake

He forgot his pads!

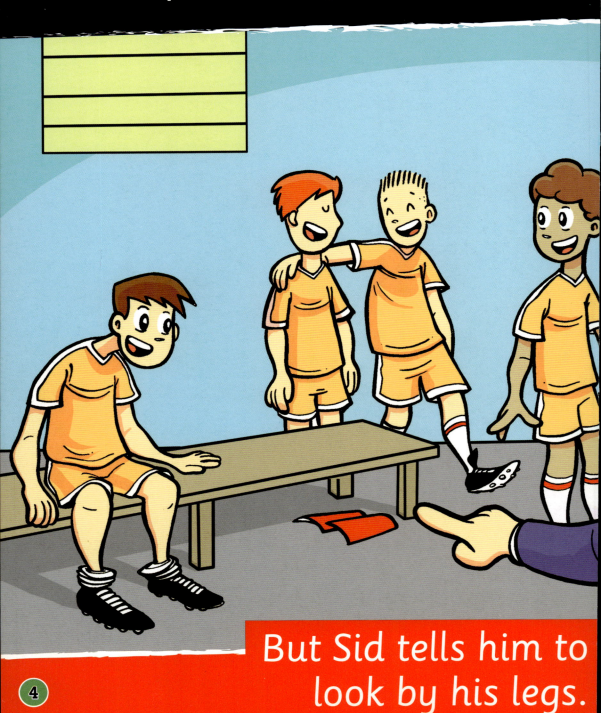

The Cats win!

Will did it!